AJI ALAN FEMI

After Death Where Do We Go?

The Path of the Soul After the Last Goodbye

First published by Aji Alan Femi 2025

First edition

ISBN: 9789334431773

This book was professionally typeset on Reedsy.
Find out more at reedsy.com

Contents

1

Acknowledgment

I am deeply grateful to the unseen forces that guided this journey: the universe, the souls who inspired these stories, and the quiet lessons that life has whispered along the way.

To my family and friends, thank you for your patience, love, and unwavering support. Your presence in my life has been a source of strength, encouragement, and inspiration.

To the readers who open this book and allow these stories to touch your heart, thank you for embracing the journey of the soul. May these pages remind you of the power of love, sacrifice, and inner light.

Finally, I offer gratitude to every soul—seen and unseen—that has walked, suffered, and loved. Your experiences have shaped these tales, and through them, your wisdom continues to inspire.

2

Introduction

Every soul carries a story, woven across lifetimes, shaped by joy, sorrow, love, and loss. Some journeys are visible, marked by the ordinary events of life; others move quietly beneath the surface, whispering lessons that only the heart can understand.

This book explores the invisible threads that connect us to nature and to the universe itself—a tapestry of souls, sacrifices, and awakenings.

Within these pages, you will meet souls who give more than they take, who love beyond reason, and who endure pain to protect and uplift others. You will witness the ways the universe guides and teaches and tests, and how the light within each of us can grow even in the darkest moments.

These are stories of love, courage, resilience, and transformation. They are reminders that life is more than what we see on the surface; it is a journey of the soul, where every ending is a beginning, and every challenge holds a hidden blessing.

May this book awaken the quiet wisdom in your heart, help you see the unseen bonds that shape our lives, and remind you that your soul's journey is sacred, unique, and always moving toward growth, understanding, and light.

3

Sacrifice That Lives On

She Hid Her Love

In a peaceful town, a girl was once seen living happily with her family, unaware of the storms that were being prepared beyond the horizon. Her days were filled with laughter; her heart was lifted by hope. When a faint illness brushed against her life, it was ignored—too much beauty was being admired for darkness to be imagined.

Marriage was given to her in her early twenties, and soon a baby boy was born—too soon, only seven months in the womb. He was made fragile, his breath tied to wires and tubes, nourished not by milk but by faith. For months, a hospital room was occupied by her presence; lullabies were sung in silence, and love poured through every glance.

Her husband, twenty-six, was employed as a driver of heavy goods along endless roads. One night, his truck was shattered by a crash. At dawn, a figure was seen crawling from the wreck—alive, though barely. His leg had been crushed, and blood was being drained like sand through broken fingers. Life was clung to, not for himself, but for his family. In that dim space between life and death, a whisper was given from his soul to hers:

"Will you care for our child? I'm not just losing blood—I'm losing myself."

It was seen by him—what no one else could see—that half of her soul had already been given away, drained by worry, sacrifice, and love. Yet she remained. For him, for their son. For what was still to come.

Months passed. Another child was conceived, though her health had been weakened. Long weeks were spent in the hospital; care was given to her healing husband. A dream of travel to Boston for better treatment was made, but fate was quicker.

A baby girl was delivered early, pink and chubby, her eyes glistening like glass. She was hidden in a towel by her grandmother, who feared the cold. Beside her limping father, she was placed, and into her small heart, strength was whispered.

Years were allowed to pass. The boy had grown strong; the father was made to walk again. But the mother began to fade. Her heart was weakened, and her medicines multiplied. Still, no truth was known by the children.

The boy's heart was filled with love for her, even when distance and sternness were shown. Small mistakes were punished; seriousness was always shown. The girl clung to her father, mistaking her mother's silence for cruelty. To them, she felt like a storm instead of a shelter.

The truth was unseen:

Only a quarter of her soul was left.

The rest had been spent to keep them alive.

Love was not hidden out of coldness—it was hidden so they would not ache when she was gone.

Then the night came that changed everything.

The children were sent to their grandmother's house. Their mother remained with her own. At midnight, a knock was heard. A message was delivered that shattered the air:

"She's gone."

Laughter of disbelief was heard from the children. She had seemed fine only hours earlier. How could someone be taken so suddenly?

But the truth had already been known to her.

She had asked her mother to wash her body and to braid her hair.

Sleep had refused her; water had been warmed and sipped slowly. Blood was coughed onto her lips. A rush was made to the hospital. On the way, her voice was heard, ashamed:

"Mum... I couldn't hold my urine."

Her mother had replied softly, "Don't worry, my child. I'll wash it later."

Machines were heard crying. Her pulse was weakened. She was moved again. A wheelchair carried what her legs could not. Her mother pleaded with the doctors, "Please, let me see her one last time." But permission was not given.

She was returned home on a stretcher, wrapped in white. Silent. Still. Gone.

Her husband was left frozen.

Her children were never allowed a goodbye.

And only then was the truth lifted like smoke from ashes:

She had known.

She had loved them with all she had.

She had hidden it—so they would not break when she left.

At the funeral, relatives were gathered and then dispersed.

Her husband was seen holding his children close, his voice breaking:

"How will I raise them without her?"

But it was done.

Through the strength of her love, it still breathed through every corner of their story.

4

A Love beyond Life

The Soul That Stayed Behind

Continuation

The children were held tightly in their father's arms as their cries were carried into the silent night, echoing like shards of broken glass. The pain of losing their mother was too heavy to be borne by hearts so small. Their tears were wiped away by trembling hands, yet the sorrow was never silenced—it returned again and again, wave after wave, too deep to escape.

Their bodies were weakened by grief, and soon they were taken to the hospital—fragile in both heart and health. Their father was seen beside them, shattered but unyielding. Their grandmother was there too, her arms opened as a cradle of comfort, as though the emptiness left behind could somehow be filled.

Above them, something unseen was stirred.

Their mother's soul had been released from her body, but her family had not been left behind. She was there—soft as wind, bright as dust in sunlight, broken yet watching. She had not vanished. She had become air.

She could not touch them.

She could not speak.

But they were seen. And they were loved.

Though seventy percent of her light had been given away—to her children first, and then to her husband—a small spark was still preserved. Through the veil of life and death, that spark was sent outward.

It was carried down like morning mist, settling gently into her son and then into her daughter.

And healing was begun.

Their coughs were eased, their fevers were cooled, and their tears, though still warm, were shed not from pain but from memory.

But her soul had become thin; too much had been given, lost. Rebirth would not be granted easily.

Some souls are returned quickly—whole, strong, burning bright.

But hers had been scattered across time: in the hospital bed, in her children's lungs, in the quiet kitchen, in every act of hidden love.

A soul so drained would not return for a hundred years.

Still, rest was denied.

Her longing to protect them remained.

So a choice was made.

With the last of her light, she wandered through mountains and cities, through young hearts and old ones, whispering silently,

"Who is strong enough to carry my love?"

And she was guided, at last, to someone new—not a stranger, not a ghost.

But a woman whose kindness was heard in her voice, whose strength was shown in her hands, and whose love was given without demand. She would not replace the mother—only continue her care.

Into this woman's heart, the mother's final breath of soul was folded.

The children were never told why she felt so familiar, why her presence seemed to glow with warmth from long ago, or why her hugs carried the scent of forgotten memories.

But somewhere deep within, beyond words, it was known:

Love had returned—not in the same form, but with the same soul.

5

The Light Within

A Daughter Awakens to Her Own Soul

Her father lived in silent pain—his leg broken, aching each night under the weight of duty. Yet he never spoke of it. He drove his heavy vehicle through endless roads, pressing the brake and accelerator with a fractured limb, swallowing pain for his children's sake. No one knew. Not even the ones he carried through life with his love and sacrifice.

Twenty years later, the truth surfaced. The daughter's heart crumbled beneath the weight of guilt. She had leaned on him, depended on him, never realizing how much it had cost.

The guilt gnawed at her spirit. How can I ever repay my parents' sacrifice? she wondered. The question echoed daily, a haunting rhythm of regret. Yet from that sorrow, a quiet fire began to grow — a longing to change.

Her soul heard her. It rose, luminous and patient, and whispered:

"How deeply do you wish to change?"

Then came distractions — temptations, comforts, the soft illusion of escape. The soul watched, aching, as she slipped again and again. Yet each time, something pulled her back — a friend's voice, a stranger's story, a sudden realization.

Gradually, her eyes opened to the truth: every wasted moment was stolen from her soul's purpose.

A battle began — not in the world, but within. Between her body's comfort and her soul's calling. The search turned inward, past noise and praise, until one morning, she found herself.

And she awoke.

She no longer waited for someone to save her.

She lit her own fire.

She built her own path.

She became her own guide.

Then she understood:

"The light I searched for outside had always been burning within me."

As her soul grew stronger, she began to meet others — other

souls also awakening, rising. Among them, unseen yet near, her mother's soul walked beside her.

Not in words, but in the courage she found.

Not in form, but in the wisdom she felt.

The mother who once left had never truly gone.

She had only become light — the light now burning in her daughter's soul.

6

The Girl I Never Met, but Always Loved

A Soul Story from Beyond the Veil

I live now in an old home. Life has taken many turns, and somehow, I've become one of its quiet souls—another story folded in sorrow and silence.

One day, twin baby boys were born here—identical in size, cry, and the light in their eyes. But whispers told of a missing third—a baby girl who should have been among them.

Their parents, crushed by poverty, faced an impossible choice. In a night filled with hushed prayers and helpless tears, they let her go—not out of heartlessness, but survival. Love had to bow before life's cruelty.

Later, I learned the baby girl had died from illness. Her fragile breath, like a candle flickering in a storm, was snuffed out before it could truly begin.

I had never seen her and never held her.

Yet something inside me shattered.

The grief struck deep and sudden, as though I had lost someone I'd always known. It made no sense—and yet it felt truer than anything.

How could I mourn so deeply for someone I had never met?

The sorrow was unreasonable, but it was real. A strange, invisible bond had formed between us—one I would not understand until much later.

By grace, I was allowed to attend her small, silent funeral.

The day was gray and cold. A thin drizzle softened the edges of the world, as if nature itself wept. The room was cramped and heavy with quiet grief. The scent of damp earth and faint incense clung to the air.

As I stood beside her still body, the world seemed to slow. The silence turned sacred. Beneath it, I felt something stir—a pulse, a whisper brushing against my soul.

I closed my eyes and reached out with my spirit, trembling yet certain.

And then... she spoke.

Not with words, but with soul.

"Do you remember me?
In a life before this one, we were best friends.
We shared everything—laughter, dreams, even silence.
But you died first, and I lived longer.
Now you were born before me... and I came too late.
I didn't get the chance to be with you again."

Her presence was soft and radiant—a light untouched by darkness. Around her, there was only purity, innocence, and a strength that reached beyond the veil.

Then she said:

"I don't want to leave you again.
I want to stay—within you.
But I cannot do this without your soul's permission.
Without full acceptance, I would fade."

Inside, I felt the weight of her sacred request.
And somehow, my soul whispered yes.

Our spirits merged—not in death, but in life.
A rare grace. A quiet miracle.

She could not live a full life in her own body, so her energy chose to continue through mine.
Her little soul entered gently, lovingly.
And now... she lives within me.

Since that day, I feel her in quiet moments.
When the night grows heavy, her light wraps around me like

a warm cloak.

Her presence isn't a burden—it's protection.

When darkness approaches, she stands before me—a shield of light, a promise kept.

Once, during a restless night, shadows crept near my window. Fear rose inside me—but her warmth blossomed within, and peace followed, soft as dawn breaking through clouds.

I never got to call her my sister.

I never saw her laugh or cry.

But she was mine—and I was hers—in another life... and now again, in this one.

"I came late," she whispered, "but not too late.

I only wanted to laugh with you again—just one lifetime more."

She may have left the world too soon, but her soul still travels with mine.

And I will carry her light wherever I go.

7

The Soul That Refused to Give Up

From Fragments to a New Life

He came from a poor background, dreaming of changing his life. Step by step, he climbed toward that dream, reaching beyond his limits. The road was filled with rejections, wounds, and quiet battles—but he never gave up.

He had a rare kind of soul—steady, focused, untouched by the noise around him. Even when storms raged, he stood firm. People began to notice. His work inspired others. But behind the applause, he fought unseen wars.

Ironically, it wasn't a great tragedy that broke him. It was something small—so small no one else noticed. A mistake, a disappointment, a moment he couldn't handle. That tiny crack grew until it shattered him.

In a single day, he ended his life.

But his soul did not die.
In the unseen world, it made a vow:

"Next time, we will not end like this."

The soul shattered into countless fragments, scattering across the air—searching for others like itself. It wandered, gathering strength, learning patience. It waited in silence, choosing carefully.

In time, the fragments fused—one soul, woven from many. A new energy was born: wiser, stronger, and unbreakable. It waited for the right parents, the right moment, and the right life.

And then, a child was born.

The boy grew up quietly, unaware of the legacy pulsing inside him.

One day, at school, there was a music contest. His friend was supposed to perform, but something went wrong. To help, the boy stepped up to the microphone—just to support him. Everyone assumed he was a contestant.

The topic: Self-Love.

He hadn't rehearsed. But when he touched the mic, something ancient stirred within him. His heart began to hum with a memory older than his body.

He sang—not as a child, but as a soul that had wandered through lifetimes:

"Because of my mistake, I lost you.
Until I die, I will help you.
Please... never leave me again."

The room froze. A hush swept through the crowd. Even he stood still, shaken by the sound of his own voice.

It wasn't just a song.
It was a soul calling out to itself—across time, across death.

People wept. They applauded through tears.
He was chosen on the spot, his path opening before him like a sunrise.

But what no one knew was this:
The soul had planned it all in silence—the song, the contest, the return.

This was the moment it had waited for across lifetimes.
This time, it would not fail.

8

The Shield That Never Fades

A Father's Eternal Vow

A restless fire was carried within the boy—fierce in form, yet tender in spirit. Life's hands were placed upon him, urging him to leave home and seek his fortune in a distant land. But destiny had been written differently. A meeting was meant to happen, and when she was encountered, his soul was stirred into remembrance. Long ago, their energies had touched; now, in this lifetime, they were drawn once more into each other's orbit. Love was awakened, a marriage was bound, and soon, a child was brought into being.

A journey abroad had been planned, yet a whisper from the unseen urged him to remain. Something mysterious was believed to surround the child's fate. So, home was stayed in, and nearby work was taken. Walls were painted by his hands, not merely for a living, but as if time itself wished to keep him close. For forty days after the birth, his presence was fixed near the fragile new life, as though a silent duty had been assigned to him by the stars.

Then came the accident. A single misstep, a hidden wire, and a fall from high above—the body was broken, and the blood was spilled. Yet the essence was not scattered. In that moment, his soul was caught between worlds, and a vow was formed. His spirit refused to depart; instead, it spread through the air like light, encircling the infant in an unseen shield. A protection was placed—one that no death could dissolve.

The ordinary path of souls was not followed. No wandering was done, no merging with the great beyond. His love kept him tethered. He became the breath that guarded the child's sleep, the quiet warmth behind every heartbeat, and the unseen strength that guided each small step. Through the years, his invisible presence nourished the child's growth.

When the child turned ten, a gentle shifting began within the father's soul. Some fragments of his energy were drawn toward other newborn bodies, starting their own journeys. Yet a part of him lingered—the part that could not let go.

Through the turning of lifetimes, the circle of love was spun again and again. His spirit took on new forms—sometimes returning as one who cared for the child, as a stranger whose eyes held a hidden knowledge. At last, rebirth was granted fully, and the father's essence found a new vessel. In one of life's strange folds, even the doctor who once watched over the child carried within them the same eternal soul.

Thus, the mystery was revealed: love does not vanish when the body falls. A soul may choose to stay, to shield, to guide, to return, and to weave itself through time until the purpose of its promise is fulfilled.

9

Fire in Her Hands

The Flame That Never Dies

She was born into a world where submission was demanded before speech could bloom. Her earliest memories were of her mother—bent over cold floors, scrubbing and polishing for those who could afford brightness, while the poor remained dim in hunger. From such a childhood, hardship was inherited, but so was defiance. A fire was lit within her—a silent promise that her life would not be chained by neglect or by poverty's shadow.

From girlhood, her eyes searched beyond the narrow street. The world's order was studied: its rules, its power, and the strange truth that those who were seen were those who were heard. Visibility was understood as strength; publicity, as the door to influence.

The boxing ring became her sanctuary. Every opponent stood as an echo of sorrow, of struggle, of the life she had outgrown. Each strike was a sentence spoken in the language of will. Her fists carried the heat of survival; her tears became steel. Through years of relentless discipline, her name was carved into the nation's memory—not only as a champion, but as a symbol. And from that symbol, politics called.

Her rise was not a climb for self alone. She carried with her the muted voices of the forgotten, the silenced, and the bent backs of her mother's generation. She became their shield, their echo, and their advocate. A man who understood her flame was met and married, and together they raised children. But fate, with its unseen patterns, took their youngest—a baby boy whose short breath became a whispering wind. His spirit was believed to remain near, guarding her dreams, sending warnings through visions of fire and fall.

When Power was crowned as president, her rule was marked by tireless service. She fought for equality, for dignity, for the right of every unseen soul to rise. Yet, as light grew around her, envy gathered its shadows. Watching eyes waited for her to fall.

One weekend was chosen for rest—a picnic planned beneath a gentle sun. Yet the night before, dreams came heavy: gunshots, betrayal, sudden stillness. Dawn erased the dream, but not the unease. Still, she moved forward, led by duty and love. And in that ordinary morning, destiny's cruel hand was revealed. A trusted friend—a beloved actress from a powerful house—turned against her. A single pull of the trigger ended a lifetime of flame. The nation was silenced; her husband stood as stone, emptied of everything but grief.

Within a month, the actress too met death—and their souls, once intertwined by fate and fury, were released into the world. Not as ghosts, but as pure energy. Their essence scattered like sparks into newborn lives, far apart yet connected by the same invisible fire.

Her son, grown and grieving, turned away from politics, refusing his inheritance of fame. Yet the fire within him—quiet, eternal—was the same.

For life, it seems, scatters its embers widely. Even in death, her flame was not extinguished; it was shared—passed on through breath, through blood, through souls yet to rise.

10

Souls Reborn, Destinies Intertwined

When Past Lives Guide the Present

Two boys were born into different worlds, yet unseen threads had already begun weaving their fates together.

The first arrived in a struggle. His father was gone before his first breath; his mother's hands were worn from endless labor, her heart heavy but unbroken. Even as an infant, he carried an unnamed fire—a restless whisper within: You are meant for more. You are meant to rise. The walls around him were cold, and neighbors passed with indifference. Children mocked or ignored him, yet the spark within only flared brighter. Often he would wander into the small courtyard, gaze upward, and imagine a life beyond those narrow streets—a courage growing silently beneath his longing.

Far away, another boy entered life wrapped in comfort. Yet

beneath that safety, a quiet resilience stirred. His gaze was steady, his movements deliberate, as though he had been born with a secret map of life's hidden paths. Teachers marveled at his intuition; friends leaned toward his calm. Even in play, an unseen gravity surrounded him—the calm of a soul that had seen much before.

Neither boy remembered what their souls had once been, yet echoes throbbed within their bones. The fire of a ruler's spirit lived inside the first. The resolve of a rebel soul breathed within the second. Though their pasts were veiled, these buried energies shaped their instincts, their choices, and their destinies.

As they grew, signs of the unseen grew stronger. The first boy spoke with quiet command, warning of dangers before they came, leading others without trying. Yet he was still a child—lonely, fearful, aching to be understood. At night, he held imagined conversations with invisible voices, voices that felt like home.

The second boy moved through life with patience beyond his years. In certain moments, his hands trembled—as if touched by memory. He loved his mother fiercely, lightening her burdens without reason, as though an ancient duty lingered within him.

Fate, patient and unyielding, guided them closer. Paths crossed like whispers—a glance in the market, a fleeting recognition in the classroom, two shadows meeting beneath the same sky. The energy between them pulsed, heavy with unfinished lessons and promises not yet fulfilled.

Then came the inevitable. A quiet room. Two hearts pounding. Breathing, trembling with anticipation, neither could name it. A gun was drawn. A trigger pulled. The first boy fell—his fire flaring one last time, confusion and calm flickering together in his fading eyes.

The second boy froze, his hands shaking—as if another's will had moved through him. Silence followed, deep and ancient. The echo of past lives reverberated between them.

It was fate—unalterable, precise, merciless.

Their bodies fell, yet the story did not end. Their souls rose beyond flesh, carrying debts that stretched across lifetimes. Their energies mingled and merged, creating a single fire awaiting rebirth.

The poor boy returned first, reborn as a soldier, sworn to protect the president with his life. Yet destiny's irony endured: in another life, that same president had been the one who ended his own. Now the protector stood over the executioner.

At first, he served faithfully. But time revealed what loyalty had hidden. The president's heart grew cruel, his hands heavy upon the weak. The cries of the people went unanswered. The soldier's soul trembled. To protect was to defend injustice; to remain silent was to betray truth. His spirit wrestled until the weight became unbearable.

Then, one day, destiny repeated itself. His hand lifted the gun. The shot rang out.

The president fell—not as an innocent, but as one who had strayed from his purpose. The soldier stood over him, neither hero nor villain, only a soul trapped in the endless exchange of fate—the killer and the killed, forever intertwined.

And so the wheel turned again. Justice did not obey reason; mercy did not always arrive in time. Souls carried their debts through centuries, binding oppressor and victim, protector and betrayer, until understanding was finally won.

Yet even as bodies fell, their fire was not extinguished. It scattered into new streams of life—awaiting birth, awaiting awakening.

And somewhere, in the quiet rhythm of the universe, a whisper endured:

"This is not the end. The souls will rise again."

11

Soul Transmission and Rebirth

When Endings Become Beginnings

Souls move like energy through the vastness of the universe. We cannot see them, yet they are always near—waiting for the right moment, the right vessel, the right life. Sometimes two streams of energy meet, and together they form a single, complete soul. That soul waits in silence until it can enter a mother's womb. When it does, a new life begins—a story with its own path, its own lesson, and its own light.

But the flow of energy is never constant. Sometimes, there are pauses—brief silences in the eternal current. Souls waiting to be reborn linger between realms, restless, their purposes incomplete. Messages ripple through the living world: some souls are called to offer part of their own energy, while others continue their journeys unaware, shining brightly in their earthly forms.

Among them, a few—compassionate and wise—choose to share. They glimpse the waiting ones and give freely, understanding that existence is not bound to one life, one body, or one time.

One such moment unfolded quietly on a busy street. Two people rode a motorbike, their minds absorbed in ordinary thought, their hearts steady in rhythm. Yet somewhere deep within, their souls sensed a call—a waiting energy needing help to return, a rebirth delayed, seeking completion.

No soul can return without divine consent. Both the Creator and the soul must agree before rebirth can unfold. But when a soul accepts the sacred challenge, it is honored in heaven's unseen balance—promised a gentler path in lives to come, peace for its selfless act.

Then fate moved. The ordinary shattered in an instant. The road curved, the wheels slipped, and time broke open. In a breath, life was taken from them—pain, surprise, and confusion flashing through their final awareness. But their essence did not die. It lifted, bright and weightless, freed from flesh and gravity.

Their energies scattered into the unseen, drifting through celestial currents. And there—where new souls waited, trembling in completion—they found purpose. Two streams met, merged, and fused into one luminous energy. Their compassion and courage became the foundation for a new life.

From that sacred union, a new soul was formed—radiant, balanced, carrying within it the memory of sacrifice and the strength of shared light. Soon, it entered the womb of a mother, beginning its story on Earth.

The ones who had given their energy did not vanish. They ascended gently, their consciousness rewarded with peace, their selfless act recorded in the eternal ledger of love.

Thus, the cycle continued. What appears to us as tragedy is often a turning of the divine wheel—a completion disguised as loss. The boys who fell that day did not disappear. Their departure became a doorway, allowing another life to begin.

And so, nothing is wasted. Every soul has a purpose. Every ending carries within it the seed of a new beginning.

Life, death, and rebirth are not separate journeys—they are one infinite rhythm, guided by God, sustained by love, and forever moving toward the next awakening.

12

The Voice That Saved Me

Finding Love Where I Never Looked

Love had long been awaited, though its path had never been known. Each day had been lived in quiet effort—friendships were sought, smiles were worn even when the heart trembled, and hope was held though rejection came again and again. It was believed that if enough kindness was shown, perhaps someone would notice. Yet the world remained unmoved; attention was given to her work, never to her heart. Presence was kept for what she offered, not for who she was.

Still, waiting continued. A dream was carried—of someone who would protect her, someone who would see her worth without proof, someone whose love would not depend on effort. Yet no one came.

The mirror reflected questions to her. Was it her beauty that was lacking? Her health? Her spirit? Each rejection was met with strength, yet every strength left another wound behind. Smiles were offered to the world, while within, a soft voice asked, "Will no one ever see me? Will no one ever love me for who I truly am?"

In time, the belief took root that her fate was different. Perhaps she had been meant only to be a companion, a helper, a fleeting presence in others' lives—useful, yet never loved deeply. Protection had been longed for, but instead, walls were built—walls so high that even love could not climb over.

What she never knew was that a voice had always been near. A soul had always walked beside her—unseen, unheard, but never absent. That soul had whispered gently, "I am here. I want your friendship. I wish to protect you. I wish to be your shield." But her eyes had searched elsewhere, and her ears had been closed to the whisper. The love that had been awaited outside had already been waiting within.

When at last her strength was gone, when despair weighed heavier than breath, when the thought of ending her life arose like a shadow over the heart, the soul broke open and cried out:

"Do not do this. I do not hate you. Even through this pain, I still seek your hand to survive. It is not too late. There is still time. You can change your life. In the next life, I may not reach you; I may not speak to you. But here and now, I am with you. I have always been with you. Please, do not let go."

Her soul had been torn because love had been sought in the outer world. Happiness had been chased in faces, in voices, and in praise—but not in the heart that lived within her. The farther she ran from herself, the more broken she became. The more she begged for others' love, the farther she drifted from her own.

And yet the truth had always been simple: when care was given to her own heart—to her mind, her body, her breath—she would no longer need to beg for love. The love she gave herself would become the healing she had been searching for. And when she was whole again, love from others would come of its own accord, gently and freely.

Her story did not have to end. It only had to begin again—not with new people, but with new eyes. The soul, her oldest friend, waited still: patient, faithful, unbroken through all pain. For the shield she had searched for in the world had never been lost. It had always lived within her.

13

The Guardian and the Shadow

When Mercy Heals the Heart

The Guardian had always been moved by the wish to improve the world. Every effort made by him came at a price, though he possessed little to give. Yet people were drawn to his goodness. They offered help freely—gifts of time, property, and money—believing that through him, life could become better.

But the Shadow looked upon it all in silence. No hand was raised, no help offered. He turned away from each burden, and in time, the people turned away from him. They admired the Guardian and despised the Shadow, never seeing how light and shadow belonged to the same day.

One day, the Guardian, worn and wounded from endless struggle, fell upon the ground. Concerned hearts gathered around him. In his weakness, he whispered, "The Shadow brought this upon me..." and closed his eyes. The words were half-breath, half-pain—but they were taken as truth.

Anger rose among the villagers. They ran to the Shadow's house, shouting blame, and before a word could be spoken, he was struck and cast away.

Days passed. The Guardian's wounds began to close, but the Shadow's spirit weakened in his lonely dwelling. That night, his soul whispered into the still air, "I could not hold myself. I have lost half of my soul. Shall I share what remains through the wind? Have I any wish left at the end of this life?"

Memories flowed like tears—memories of words misunderstood, of silence mistaken for guilt, of good unseen.

Meanwhile, the Guardian continued his mission. His wealth was given away to build for others—schools, shelters, and sanctuaries. Those who opposed him came to bargain: "Let us share your property. Together we will prosper."

But he refused. And in their fury, they struck him again.

In that moment, it was the Shadow who appeared. Without hesitation, he lifted the wounded Guardian and carried him to safety, though his own strength failed, and he collapsed by the threshold.

Later, when the Shadow awoke, he tended to his pain with simple herbs. Visitors came, questioning him about the Guardian, but his voice was faint. Misunderstanding followed once more—suspicion in place of truth, blame instead of gratitude.

Soon after, the Guardian tried to rise from his bed. He opened his mouth to speak—to tell the truth, to clear the Shadow's name—but his strength betrayed him. The machine beside him fell silent. His soul slipped away, whispering, "I could not finish speaking... they misunderstood..."

When word reached the Shadow, he bowed his head in grief. "He died because of me," he murmured. "Every word unsaid, every truth unseen, has become my burden."

That night, sleep fled from him. His heart trembled beneath the weight of sorrow.

But then, there in the stillness, light appeared. The Shadow's soul, now radiant and free, came forth. A voice of mercy spoke through the light:

"I forgive you."

And in that moment, healing filled the air. The Guardian's spirit, now bathed in forgiveness, returned briefly—glowing, peaceful, and redeemed. Through that light, it was shown that even in death, forgiveness may awaken life, and mercy may mend what pain had broken.

For when the body ends, the soul carries the memory of every deed. Yet mercy, when given or received, heals beyond all worlds—restoring peace where once there was only grief.

14

The Treasure Hidden in Nature

The Tree That Gave Her Life

When we surrender ourselves to the universe, to nature, to life itself, we begin to see everyone equally, and every goodness comes to us naturally.

She understood this truth only after misfortune touched her life. Once, she believed in family, in society, and in the order of the world. But when fate turned against her, all she had vanished—property, shelter, security—lost in a single cruel moment. Within a week, she was alone on the streets, searching for help from those she once called her own. No one came.

The city, once familiar, became a wilderness of cold indifference. So she wandered to the countryside, seeking survival among the silent fields.

Hunger gnawed at her belly. Thirst burned her lips. Days blurred into nights, and her body weakened. Darkness closed in as she fell to the earth, powerless. Her prayer rose not in words but in the silent language of the soul—a cry to God, to the universe, to the heart of nature itself.

Then the rain came—soft at first, then strong, washing away her despair. Water gathered around her; she drank what she could, and in her exhaustion, drifted into sleep beneath the whispering leaves.

When she awoke, the world was different. A tree towered above her, its roots holding the earth like arms of compassion. Beneath its shade lay a small cluster of fruit, fresh and glowing as though placed by unseen hands. She ate, and life returned to her veins.

Gratitude filled her heart. She understood then that the true treasure of life is hidden in nature. When we stop chasing the world and instead accept nature's quiet gifts, every day becomes enough.

From that moment on, she lived in harmony with the natural world. Her body healed, her mind found peace, and her soul grew strong and wise.

Years later, she returned to the city and found many old, hungry souls—people forgotten by the world. She welcomed them without question, giving them food, shelter, and kindness. Among them, she recognized two faces she had long lost—her own parents, aged and weary. Without bitterness, she took them in, and together they thrived once more in the countryside, protected by the wisdom and generosity of nature.

In the quiet evenings, as the wind whispered through the trees, she realized the truth: when we surrender our souls to nature, the universe answers. Every fear, every need, every sorrow finds resolution.

The treasures of life do not lie in wealth or status—they rest gently in the patient, nurturing arms of the natural world.

15

Love Beyond Romantic

The Cat of Four Souls

A pair of souls wandered toward the Wells of Creation—the place where new life is born from the quiet breath of the universe.

But the air was thin that day. Creation had slowed; only fragments of unfinished souls drifted in the wind. The pair waited through many cycles—through silence, through starlight—until, at last, a new soul began to take shape.

When their child arrived, joy overflowed within them. Yet, in the same instant, sorrow began its silent unfolding. The mother's light dimmed; the father stood trembling beside her, unable to understand why joy could hurt so deeply. He felt a storm rising—something unseen—and, with his final strength, he sent their newborn soul away to a safe place among the winds of time. Soon after, both parents faded into the air, their love dissolving into invisible warmth.

No one knew why they vanished so suddenly. Days passed, and even the sibling soul, once glowing nearby, scattered into the vastness. The newborn remained—fragile, flickering, alone.

Then one wandering soul came upon the child and stayed close, shielding it from the cold spaces between worlds. The young soul felt happiness again—brief but bright. Yet happiness, in that realm, never lingered long. The protector soul, too, began to fade, whispering its last warmth into the child's fragile light.

The newborn cried into the emptiness:

"Why does everyone leave me alone? Am I cursed? Am I a demon?"

But the truth was tender and unseen. All four souls—the mother, the father, the sibling, and the stranger—had given their essence to save the child.

The mother, knowing no strength remained in the air, gave the last of her light. The father, unaware of her act, gave his as well. Their love—too vast to measure—became their undoing. The sibling soul followed, offering what little remained of its spark. Only a final piece was missing—and the wandering stranger, moved by unseen compassion, gave that too.

Time flowed gently forward. The child's soul grew, wandering through solitude, whispering into the silence for those who had vanished.

One night, beneath a sky of still stars, a cat appeared. Its eyes glowed with warmth and memory. The young soul felt something stir—a recognition too deep for words.

Then it understood. The cat was not a stranger.

It was love reborn—the four souls, merged and gentle, returned to comfort the one they had saved.

They had taken form again, not as voices or light, but as a heartbeat beside the lonely—a quiet companion through every dark hour.

From that day, the soul and the cat stayed together. Their bond was not of romance or reason but of something older—the memory of sacrifice, the echo of love beyond death.

And thus, the answer came softly, like dawn upon the wind:

After death, we do not go away—we only change our shape
To stay near the ones we love.

16

The Soul's Journey

Miracles Hidden in Everyday Life

The universe is the God that shapes our happiness and sadness. Some souls have not yet experienced much, so nature trains them—through joy and through pain—to grow stronger and wiser. Every challenge helps the soul become humble and grateful. Every soul is unique, carrying its own lessons and emotions. Nothing truly lies in our hands, so there is no need to worry. Everything happens for a reason. Learn from every incident, but never think of ending your soul's journey—for we have no right to harm it. Give yourself time to face your problems; they are not here to destroy you but to teach you understanding.

Every day may seem the same, yet each day hides a small miracle—a quiet blessing waiting to be found. Do not wait for a better life for your soul; create moments that heal it now. If you keep waiting, your existence loses meaning. It is never too late to be calm and to seek where your peace is hidden.

Happiness does not come from another soul—it begins within. Be loyal to yourself. Make your soul happy until it is ready to scatter into the air and return to the universe. Never compare your soul with another, for every soul has a different purpose. Do not judge or overthink. Find your purpose and light it along your soul's path.

Take care of yourself, for the soul lives within your body. Care for your body's health, for it carries your soul through this lifetime. Keep your mind peaceful, and your soul will rest easy—always guiding you toward the right choices in life.

17

Conclusion

Life is the whisper of the soul, a journey through unseen realms where love, loss, and awakening intertwine. Every heartbeat carries a lesson, every tear a quiet blessing, every smile a spark of light that lingers beyond the moment.

Through these stories, we have walked with souls who endure, who sacrifice, and who rise again and again. We have seen that love is never lost, that even in absence, it transforms, protects, and guides. Souls do not vanish—they scatter, merge, and return, weaving an eternal tapestry of connection and purpose.

May you carry these truths within you: that your soul is unique, luminous, and eternal; that happiness begins within; and that even the deepest shadows hold the promise of light. Life's trials are not to break you, but to awaken the strength and wisdom already dwelling in your heart.

And as you journey onward, remember: every ending is a

beginning, every loss a seed of growth, and every breath a chance to honor your soul. Embrace your path with courage, gratitude, and love, for the universe watches, guiding you gently toward the light that has always been inside you.

18

Appendix

Understanding the Journey of Souls, Lessons, and Life

This appendix provides additional insight into the concepts, characters, and spiritual lessons explored throughout this book. It is meant to guide readers in connecting the threads of stories, souls, and the wisdom they carry.

1. The Nature of the Soul

Every soul is unique, carrying its own lessons, strengths, and challenges.

Souls travel across lifetimes, learning, healing, and growing through experiences.

Even when physical life ends, the soul continues, often guiding or protecting others in unseen ways.

2. Cycles of Life, Death, and Rebirth

Life is a continuous cycle: birth, growth, challenges, death, and rebirth.

Souls may scatter, merge, or transfer fragments to help new lives.

Rebirth allows lessons unfinished in previous lives to continue, giving souls another chance to fulfill their purpose.

3. Soul Connections

Souls often carry bonds that transcend lifetimes: love, friendship, mentorship, or protection.

These bonds can appear as instinct, recognition, or guidance, even without conscious memory.

Examples in the book:

A mother's soul protects her children after death.

A soul merging with another to provide companionship, guidance, or love.

4. Lessons from Struggles

Challenges are growth opportunities. They teach humility, patience, gratitude, and understanding.

Every incident, even pain, contributes to a soul's development.

Waiting for happiness outside oneself is futile; true peace and love begin within.

5. Symbols and Recurring Themes

Symbol Meaning in the Book

Light is the essence of a soul: guidance, love, hope

Fire, determination, passion, courage, and inner strength

Nature Healing, grounding, and connection to the universe

Cats/Animals Spiritual guardians, love reborn, invisible guidance

Music Soul expression, memory of past lives, emotional healing

6. Reflections and Practices

Pause daily to reflect on small miracles around you; they are signs of the soul's growth.

Nurture your body and mind—they carry your soul.

Practice self-love and patience; your soul's journey is personal and unique.

Observe synchronicity or coincidences—they may be guidance from unseen energies.

7. Character and Soul Guide

Chapter/Story Key Soul Lesson

- A Love Beyond Life Sacrifice: Eternal love, Protection beyond death
- The Light Within Awakening: Self-realization, Inner guidance
- The Girl I Never Met Soul Bonds: Love beyond Physical Presence
- The Soul That Refused to Give Up: Persistence, Learning

from mistakes, Rebirth

- Fire in Her Hands: Courage, Resilience, Carrying the legacy of struggle
- Souls Reborn: Destinies Intertwined Fate, Justice, The cycle of life and rebirth
- Soul Transmission and Rebirth Compassion: Generosity of spirit, New beginnings
- The Voice That Saved Me: Self-love: Recognizing guidance within
- The Guardian and the Shadow Forgiveness: Mercy, Unseen protection
- The Treasure Hidden in Nature Harmony with life: Nature as teacher
- Love beyond Romantic Sacrifice: Love beyond form, Guardianship

19

From the Author to the Reader

Dear Reader,

This book is a journey—a journey not only through stories but also through the unseen paths of the soul. Each chapter is a reflection of life's mysteries: love, loss, courage, and the quiet strength that guides us even when we cannot see it.

I invite you to read not only with your eyes but also with your heart. Let the stories speak to the hidden corners of your soul, the lessons your spirit already knows, and the hope that life, death, and rebirth are part of a continuous cycle of growth and love.

This is not just a book of stories; it is a mirror for your own journey. May you find patience for your struggles, gratitude for your blessings, and courage to follow the light within yourself.

Thank you for allowing these words to enter your life. May they inspire you to honor your own soul, cherish the souls around you, and recognize that even in the unseen, love never truly fades.

With gratitude,
Aji Alan Femi

20

A Call to Action

Dear Reader,

The stories you have read are more than tales—they are invitations. An invitation to listen to your own soul, to honor the unseen, and to recognize the love, strength, and light within you.

Take a moment each day to pause, reflect, and nurture your inner self. Spread kindness, understanding, and compassion to those around you. Your actions, no matter how small, ripple through the lives of others and shape the world in ways you may never see.

Do not wait for another life to begin. Begin now. Love deeply, forgive freely, and live intentionally. Share your light, protect your soul, and help others awaken to theirs.

Your journey is your own—but the universe is always watching, guiding, and waiting for you to step into your fullest self.

Rise. Shine. Transform.

21

Thank You

To all the readers who have opened these pages and walked alongside these souls—thank you. Your time, attention, and heart mean more than words can capture.

To my family, friends, and mentors—your support and love have made this journey possible.

And to the universe, for the whispers of inspiration that guide every word—I am forever grateful.

May these stories bring light, reflection, and a gentle reminder that every soul carries a story worth honoring.

22

About the Author

Aji Alan Femi is a passionate storyteller and seeker of life's deeper truths. Through their writing, they explore the hidden connections between souls, the lessons of love, loss, and resilience, and the mystical threads that guide our journeys. Their works invite readers to reflect, feel, and awaken the light within themselves.

When not writing, Aji Alan Femi connects with readers and dreamers on Instagram @ajialanfemi and welcomes heartfelt conversations at ajialanfemi369@gmail.com.

www.ingramcontent.com/pod-product-compliance
Lightning Source LLC
Chambersburg PA
CBHW062202160726
48282CB00027B/960
* 9 7 8 9 3 3 4 4 3 1 7 7 3 *